GW01445075

이 책이 속한

This Book belongs to:

....

....

PA PPU DA

바 쁘 다

to be Busy

Printed in Great Britain
by Amazon

79156562R00070